AnneXe

D0433110

Welcome to *AnneXe*, your personal *Formule X* kit for easier learning!

AnneXe is divided into three sections:

Use *AnneXe* whenever you need to for learning and for revision.

Advice for parents

Whether you know some French or not, you can help your child with their homework in the following ways:

- help him/her decide when to do homework and try to provide a quiet area for it.

- ask your child to teach you some French.

- check that homework is completed and that enough time has been spent on it.

- praise effort and progress.

- read the advice on the next page with your child and use the suggested techniques together. Depending on the topic or what work has been done in class, the teacher might ask your child to learn:

- what some new French words mean
- what the words mean and how to say them in French
- what the words mean and how to say and spell them correctly.

All the new language is recorded on a home cassette to help with pronunciation.

● if your child has access to a computer, he/she may wish to build up a vocabulary database.

If you do know some French, you can:

● discuss how to go about certain tasks.

● check that you child has understood corrections done in class.

● help with oral practice, such as rehearsing a dialogue or learning a poem by heart.

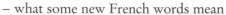

How to learn new words

You really know and understand a French word (or phrase) once you know:

- what it means when you hear it
- what it means when you see it
- how to say it in French from memory
- how to write it in French from memory.

The more you practise in class <u>and</u> at home, the more successful you will be.

Here are a few learning tips:

a Listen to one new French word or phrase at a time on your home cassette, say what it means in English, then check your answer in *AnneXe*.

b Look at a French word or phrase in *AnneXe*, pronounce it from memory, then check with your home cassette.

c Look at an English word or phrase in *AnneXe*, try to say the French from memory, then listen to it on cassette and repeat it.

d Look at an English word or phrase in *AnneXe*, write it in French from memory, then check.

With the help of *Cahier X* and your teacher, you will discover even more ways of learning new words. Good luck!

DiX sur DiX sums up the main learning objectives that appear in the Student's Book.

You can use *DiX sur DiX* to check on your progress at the end of each *Formule X* Unit. To help you use *DiX sur DiX*, here are some suggestions based on the learning objectives for Unit 1 (see *AnneXe* p 5).

Can you...

...carry out simple conversations when meeting people?

...ask and understand who someone is?

● either on your own or with a friend or parent, say as many useful words and phrases as you can remember. Do some more practice with *AnneXe* and your home cassette if you can't remember them all.

● make up some mini dialogues, either on your own or with a friend or parent.

● also practise in writing, checking against *AnneXe* afterwards.

...use and understand the alphabet?

● say the alphabet from memory, using your home cassette for checking.

● write down the letters of the alphabet in a jumbled-up order and check whether you can still say them accurately.

● ask someone to say a letter of the alphabet in French. You can then write it down and show you understand.

...understand simple instructions?

● check that you can still do activity 1 on p 12 of the Student's Book without hesitation.

...use *AnneXe*?

● check once again what each section does, with the help of the contents list on p 1.

...remember some useful techniques for learning and working better?

● browse though Unit 1 of the Student's Book again to spot some useful techniques. This will also help you remember the written instructions used in the activities more easily.

...remember things you didn't know about France?

● do some brainstorming with a friend. Take another look at p14 of the Student's Book.

Glossaire: Unités 1–14

Salut! pages 6–7

Salut	Hello/Hi
Bonjour	Hello/Good morning/Good afternoon
Je m'appelle Susan.	My name is Susan.
Et toi?	And your name is?
Tu t'appelles John?	Is your name John?
Tu t'appelles comment?	What's your name?
Tu t'appelles John ou Paul?	Is your name John or Paul?
A-B-C-D-E-F-G-H-I-J	

Ça va? pages 8–9

Ça va?	How are you/Are you alright?
Très bien, merci.	Very well, thank you.
Oui, ça va, merci.	Yes, I am alright, thank you.
Bof... oui et non.	Well... yes and no.
Et toi?	And you?
Moi?	Me?
Au revoir	Goodbye
Salut	Hello/Goodbye
K-L-M-N-O-P-Q-R-S-T	

Ça s'écrit comment? pages 10–11

C'est qui?	Who is this?
C'est...	It's...
Je ne sais pas.	I don't know.
Monsieur...	Mister...
Madame...	Mrs...
Mademoiselle...	Miss...
Ça s'écrit comment?	How is it spelt?
Ça s'écrit...	It's spelt...
U-V-W-X-Y-Z	

DiX sur DiX!

Can you…
… carry out simple conversations when meeting people?
… ask and understand who someone is?
… use and understand the alphabet?
… understand simple instructions?
… use *AnneXe*?
… remember some useful techniques for learning and working better?
… remember things you didn't know about France?

B-O-N-J-O-U-R

Un, deux, trois... *pages 16–17*

un	1
deux	2
trois	3
quatre	4
cinq	5
six	6
sept	7
huit	8
neuf	9
dix	10
plus	more/plus
moins	less/minus

Tu habites où? *pages 18–19*

Tu habites où?	Where do you live?
J'habite à Leeds.	I live in Leeds.
J'habite en France.	I live in France.
J'habite en Angleterre.	I live in England.
J'habite en Ecosse.	I live in Scotland.
J'habite en Irlande.	I live in Ireland.
J'habite en Irlande du Nord.	I live in Northern Ireland.
J'habite <u>au</u> pays de Galles.	I live in Wales.
C'est bien?	Is it alright?
C'est bien, Leeds?	Is Leeds alright?
Ah oui, c'est super!	Ah yes, it's great!
Oui, ça va/Oui, c'est bien.	Yes, it's alright.
Oh non, c'est nul!	Oh no, it's awful!

Tu as quel âge?

onze	11
douze	12
treize	13
quatorze	14
quinze	15
seize	16
dix-sept	17
dix-huit	18
dix-neuf	19
vingt	20
Tu as quel âge?	How old are you?
J'ai onze ans	I'm 11
J'ai douze ans	I'm 12

DiX sur DiX!

Can you ...
... use and understand numbers 1–20?
... give your age and ask others theirs?
... say where you live and ask others where they live?
... say whether you like where you live and ask others what they think about where they live?
... understand more instructions?
... use à/en/au accurately before towns and countries?
... remember more useful techniques for learning and working better?
... remember more about France?

Détails personnels 2

sept

7

Tu as un crayon? pages 26–27

Tu as …?	Do you have …?
Oui, j'ai …	Yes, I have …
un cahier	an/one exercise book
des cahiers	(some) exercise books
deux cahiers	two exercise books
un crayon	a/one pencil
un livre	a/one book
un stylo	a/one pen
un carnet	a/one notebook
un dictionnaire	a/one dictionary
Je n'ai pas de stylo.	I don't have a biro.
Non, mais j'ai …	No, but I have …

Je voudrais … pages 28–29

Qu'est-ce que c'est?	What is it?
C'est …	It's …
Je voudrais …	I'd like …
s'il te plaît/s'il vous plaît	please
une feuille	a/one sheet of paper
deux feuilles	two sheets of paper
des feuilles	sheets of paper
une gomme	a/one rubber
une règle	a/one ruler
une craie	a/one piece of chalk
une cassette	a/one cassette
et	and
Désolé(e)	Sorry
Oui, voilà.	Yes, here you are.
Merci	Thank you

Qu'est-ce que tu fais?	What are you doing?/ What do you do?
Je dessine.	I'm drawing/I draw.
Je pratique un dialogue.	I'm practising/I practise a dialogue.
Je corrige un exercice.	I'm correcting/I correct an exercise.
Je prépare...	I'm preparing/I prepare …
Je regarde une photo.	I'm looking at/I look at a photo.
Je recopie...	I'm copying up…/I copy up…
J'apprends un poème.	I'm learning/I learn a poem.
Je fais un poster.	I'm doing/I do a poster.
Je lis un exemple.	I'm reading/I read an example.

Di✗ sur Di✗!

Can you …
… ask what something is?
… ask for objects and respond when others ask you for something?
… say which classroom objects you have or don't have?
… say what you are doing in class and ask others about what they're doing?
… recognise nouns and verbs?
… understand about gender (masculine/feminine)?
… use nouns (singular/plural) with articles *un/une/des*?
… remember more useful techniques for learning and working better?
… remember more about France?

En classe

3

Ma famille et moi 4

Tu as des frères ou des sœurs?   pages 30–31

Tu as des frères ou des sœurs?	Do you have brothers or sisters?
J'ai …	I have …
un frère/deux frères	one brother/two brothers
un demi-frère	one half-brother
deux demi-frères	two half-brothers
une sœur/deux sœurs	one sister/two sisters
une demi-sœur	one half-sister
deux demi-sœurs	two half-sisters
un beau-frère	one stepbrother
une belle-sœur	one stepsister
Non, mais j'ai …	No, but I've got …
Je suis fils unique.	I am an only child. (boy)
Je suis fille unique.	I am an only child. (girl)
Tu es fils/fille unique?	Are you an only child?

Qu'est-ce que tu fais à la maison?   pages 30–31

Qu'est-ce que tu fais à la maison?	What do you do at home?
Je regarde la télévision.	I watch TV.
J'écoute des CD.	I listen to CDs.
J'aide mon père.	I help my father.
J'aide ma mère.	I help my mother.
Je joue avec mon frère/ma sœur.	I play with my brother/my sister.
Je joue sur mon ordinateur.	I play on my computer.
Je surfe sur Internet.	I surf the Internet.
Je fais mes devoirs.	I do my homework.
J'apprends mes leçons.	I learn my work.

Tu joues …?	Do you play …?
Tu travailles …?	Do you work …?
seul	alone (masculine)
seule	alone (feminine)
Tu joues avec qui?	Who do you play with?
Tu joues souvent?	Do you often play?
Je joue souvent …	I often play …
Je travaille quelquefois …	I sometimes work …
Je regarde rarement la télévision …	I rarely watch TV …
avec mon chien	with my dog
avec mes copains	with my friends (all boys, or boys and girls)
avec mes copines	with my friends (all girls)

*Di**X** sur Di**X**!*

Can you …

… say what brothers and sisters you have and ask others about theirs?

… say what you do at home and how often, and ask others about what they do?

… say with whom you do certain things and ask others?

… use possessives *mon/ma/mes* accurately?

… understand about infinitives (*-er* endings)?

… use verbs with *je* and *tu* correctly?

… remember more useful techniques for learning and working better?

… remember more about France?

Ma famille et moi 4

onze

11

Lundi, mardi ...

lundi	Monday
mardi	Tuesday
mercredi	Wednesday
jeudi	Thursday
vendredi	Friday
samedi	Saturday
dimanche	Sunday
C'est mardi aujourd'hui?	Is it Tuesday today?
Non, ce n'est pas mardi.	No, it isn't Tuesday.
Non, c'est jeudi.	No, it's Thursday.
vingt et un	21
vingt-deux	22
vingt-trois...	23...
... vingt-neuf	... 29
trente	30
trente et un	31

Quelle est la date?

janvier	January
février	February
mars	Mars
avril	April
mai	May
juin	June
juillet	July
août	August
septembre	Septembre
octobre	Octobre
novembre	November
décembre	December
Quelle est la date?	What's the date?
C'est le 1er (premier) mars	It's 1st March.
C'est le 3 décembre.	It's 3rd December.
mercredi 14 juillet	Wednesday 14th July

Tu as anglais le mardi?	Do you have English on Tuesdays?
J'ai anglais le lundi	I have English on Mondays
Je n'ai pas…	I haven't got/I don't have…
anglais	English
dessin	art
français	French
géo/géographie	geography
histoire	history
informatique	IT
maths	maths
musique	music
sciences	science
sport	P.E./games
techno/technologie	design and technology
(éducation civique et sociale)	(PSE)
(éducation religieuse)	(RE)
(allemand)	(German)
(espagnol)	(Spanish)

*Di**X** sur Di**X**!*

Can you …
… use and understand numbers up to 31?
… use and understand days and months?
… say and ask what the date is?
… say what school subjects you do on what days, and ask others about what they do?
… understand more instructions?
… look up verbs in a glossary (-er and -re endings)?
… find your way round a bilingual dictionary?
… remember more useful techniques for learning and working better?
… remember more about France?

Au collège 5

Mes animaux 6

Tu as un animal à la maison?	Do you/have you got a pet?
Oui, j'ai…	Yes, I have…
un chat	a cat
des chats/deux chats	cats/two cats
un chien	a dog
un cobaye	a guinea pig
un hamster	a hamster
un lapin	a rabbit
un poisson	a fish
un oiseau/des oiseaux	a bird/birds
une gerbille	a gerbil
une tortue	a tortoise
une souris/des souris	a mouse/mice
Je n'ai pas de chat.	I haven't got a cat.
Je n'ai pas d'animal.	I haven't got a pet.

Mon chat Tigger est…	My cat Tigger is…
Ma souris n'est pas…	My mouse isn't…
Mes poissons sont…	My fish are…
Mes tortues ne sont pas…	My tortoises aren't…
très…	very…
rapide(s)	fast
calme(s)	calm, quiet
drôle(s)	funny
féroce(s)	fierce
bête(s)	silly, stupid

Ton chat est drôle?	Is your cat funny?
Ta tortue est…?	Is your tortoise…?
Tes poissons sont…?	Are your fish…?
Tu aimes les animaux?	Do you like animals?
J'adore les gerbilles.	I love/I adore gerbils.
J'aime beaucoup…	I like … a lot.
J'aime…	I like …
Je n'aime pas beaucoup…	I don't like … much.
Je n'aime pas…	I don't like …
Je n'aime pas du tout…	I don't like … at all.
Je préfère…	I prefer…

Di**X** sur Di**X**!

Can you …

… say what pets you have or don't have and ask others what pets they have?

… say what your pets are like and ask others what their pets are like?

… use adjectives in the plural?

… use some nouns with irregular plurals?

… use possessives *ton/ta/tes* accurately?

… look up French nouns in a dictionary?

… remember more useful techniques for learning and working better?

… remember more about France?

Mes animaux 6

Je travaille, Je travaille...

Qu'est-ce que c'est? pages 66–67

Qu'est-ce que c'est?	What is this?
C'est...	It is...
le magnétophone	the cassette player
le tableau	the board
la craie	the chalk
la table	the table
la chaise	the chair
la porte	the door
la fenêtre	the window
la brosse	the board duster
l'écran	the screen
l'ordinateur	the computer

Comptez! pages 68–69

quarante	40
cinquante	50
soixante	60
quarante et un	41
quarante-deux	42
quarante-trois	43
La musique, c'est où?	Where is music?
Les maths, c'est où?	Where is maths?
C'est en salle 40 (quarante)	It's in room 40
Il y a...?	Is there...?
Il y a...	There is...

C'est à quelle heure? pages 70–71

La géo, c'est à quelle heure?	What time is geography?
La géo, c'est à…	Geography is at…
C'est à…	It's at…
une heure/deux heures	one o'clock/two o'clock
trois heures cinq	3.05
dix heures trente	10.30
neuf heures quarante	9.40
Tu as sciences à quelle heure?	What time have you got science?
J'ai sciences à…	I've got science at…

Di✗ sur Di✗!

Can you …

… name and understand more classroom objects?

… use and understand numbers up to 69?

… say in what rooms lessons are and ask others?

… say what time lessons are and ask others?

… use articles *le/la/l'/les* accurately?

… look up verbs in a dictionary?

… remember more useful techniques for learning and working better?

… remember more about France?

Mon frère a neuf ans pages 76–77

Ton frère s'appelle comment?	What's your brother's name?
Il s'appelle…	His name is…/He's called…
Ta sœur s'appelle comment?	What's your sister's name?
Elle s'appelle…	Her name is…/She's called…
Ton frère a quel âge?	How old is your brother?
Mon frère a 12 ans/	My brother is 12/
Il a 12 ans	He's 12
Ta sœur a quel âge?	How old is your sister?
Ma sœur a 11 ans/	My sister is 11/
Elle a 11 ans	She's 11

Ma sœur n'est pas timide! pages 78–79

Ton frère est comment?	What's your brother like?
Ta sœur est comment?	What's your sister like?
Il/Elle est…	He is/She is…
assez…	fairly…
très…	very…
timide	shy
amusant, amusante	funny (= drôle)
embêtant, embêtante	annoying
bruyant, bruyante	noisy
élégant, élégante	smart
petit, petite	small
grand, grande	tall
bavard, bavarde	talkative
intelligent, intelligente	intelligent
Il/Elle n'est pas…	He isn't/She isn't…

Ton frère/Ta sœur aime…?	Does your brother/sister like …?
Il/Elle aime…?	Does he/she like …?
Il/Elle aime aussi…?	Does he/she also like …?
le sport	sports
la télé	TV
le cinéma	the cinema/going to the cinema
la lecture	reading
les jeux vidéo	video games
la musique	musique
la danse	dancing

DiX sur DiX!

Can you …

… give your brothers and sisters' names and ages and ask others?

… say what they are like and ask others?

… say what hobbies you or others like and ask others about their hobbies?

… use adjectives in the feminine?

… use adverbs (*assez/très*) to give more precise descriptions?

… use regular -*er* verbs with *je/tu/il/elle* in the present tense?

… use *avoir* and *être* with *je/tu/il/elle* in the present tense?

… remember more useful techniques for learning and working better?

… remember more about France?

Mes frères, mes sœurs…et moi! 8

J'ai fini! pages 86–87

C'est quel exercice?	Which exercise is it?
C'est quelle page?	Which page is it?
Comment?	Pardon?
Je ne comprends pas.	I don't understand.
J'ai fini!	I've finished!
J'ai oublié mon stylo.	I've forgotten my pen.
Je peux travailler avec Tom?	Can I work with Tom?
Je peux changer de place?	Can I move?
Je peux aller aux toilettes?	Can I go to the toilet?

Je travaille avec qui? pages 88–89

Tu travailles avec qui?	Who are you working with?
Je peux travailler…?	Can I work…?
Tu peux travailler…?	Can you work…?
Il peut travailler…?	Can he work…?
Elle peut travailler…?	Can she work…?
avec moi	with me
avec nous	with us
avec toi	with you (singular)
avec vous	with you (plural)
D'accord	OK
C'est à qui?	Whose turn is it?
C'est à moi./C'est à toi.	It's my turn./It's your turn.
Ça va?	Is it alright?
Oui, ça va.	Yes, it's alright.
Non, c'est faux	No, it's wrong
Un point!	One point!

Tu aimes…?	Do you like…?
… les chansons	… songs
… les raps	… raps
… la grammaire	… grammar
… le vocabulaire	… vocabulary
… le travail en groupe	… group work
… le travail oral	… oral work
… le travail écrit	… written work
J'aime ça.	I like it./I like that.
Je n'aime pas ça	I don't like it./I don't like that.
Pourquoi?	Why?
Parce que c'est…	Because it is…
Parce que ce n'est pas…	Because it isn't…
facile	easy
difficile	difficult
intéressant	interesting
ennuyeux	boring
fatigant	tiring

*Di*X *sur Di*X*!*

Can you …
- … deal with everyday classroom matters in French?
- … conduct pair or group activities in French?
- … give and justify opinions on school subjects and activities?
- … ask others for their opinions?
- … make longer sentences using *parce que*?
- … use *je peux/tu peux/il peut/elle peut* + infinitive?
- … use verbs of like and dislike + infinitive?
- … remember more useful techniques for learning and working better?
- … remember more about France?

Une classe active! 9

C'est quand, ton anniversaire? *pages 30–31*

C'est quand, ton anniversaire?	When is your birthday?
Mon anniversaire, c'est le le 3 mai.	My birthday is on 3rd May.
C'est le 1er avril (le premier avril).	It's on 1st April.
Qu'est-ce que c'est, ton cadeau idéal?	What is your ideal present?
Mon cadeau idéal, c'est...	My ideal present is...
un ordinateur	a computer
un CD	a CD
un poster de Michael Owen	a poster of Michael Owen
une platine laser	a CD player
une peluche	a soft toy
une console vidéo	a games console
des vêtements	(some) clothes

On joue? *pages 98–99*

Tu joues...?	Would you play...?
... au Monopoly avec moi?	... Monopoly with me?
... au babyfoot avec moi?	... table football with me?
... au Scrabble avec nous?	... Scrabble with us?
... au Cluedo avec nous?	... Cluedo with us?
Pourquoi?	Why?
Pourquoi pas?	Why not?
Le Cluedo, c'est trop lent.	Cluedo is too slow.
C'est assez...	It's fairly...
C'est très...	It's very...
Ce n'est pas assez rapide.	It isn't quick enough.
Ce n'est pas très facile.	It isn't very easy.
Ce n'est pas trop difficile.	It isn't too difficult.

C'est comment, Pâques en France?
pages 100–101

C'est comment, Pâques en France?	What is Easter like in France?
On décore des œufs.	We/People decorate eggs.
On écrit des cartes.	We/People write cards.
On offre des œufs en chocolat.	We/People give chocolate eggs
On travaille le vendredi.	We/People work on the Friday.
On ne travaille pas le lundi.	We/People don't work on the Monday.
On invite la famille.	We/People invite the family.
On va à l'église.	We/People go to church.
On mange beaucoup.	We/People eat a lot.

DiX sur DiX!

Can you …

… say when your birthday is and ask others?
… say what your ideal present is and ask others?
… say what games you like or don't like to play, and why?
… use *jouer au…* and *aimer le…* accurately?
… use verbs with *on* in the present tense?
… use the present tense singular of regular -er verbs, as well as *avoir, être, s'appeler,* and *pouvoir*?
… remember more useful techniques for learning and working better?
… remember more about France?

Festivités 10

vingt-trois

23

Mes loisirs

Tu sors souvent? pages 106–107

un cinéma	a cinema
un parc	a park
un club des jeunes	a youth club
un centre sportif	a sports centre
un centre commercial	a shopping centre
un centre-ville	a town centre
un bowling	a bowling alley
Tu sors souvent?	Do you often go out?
Je sors souvent.	I often go out.
Je sors rarement.	I rarely go out.
Tu vas où?	Where do you go?
Je vais quelquefois…	I sometimes go …
Je vais souvent…	I often go …
Je vais rarement…	I rarely go …
… au cinéma, au parc, etc.	… to the cinema, to the park, etc.

Tu fais du sport? pages 108–109

Tu fais du sport?	Do you do sport?
Tu joues…?	Do you play/you play…?
Je joue…	I play…
au football	football
au rugby	rugby
au basket	basketball
au cricket	cricket
au hockey	hockey
au tennis	tennis
au volley-ball	volleyball
au golf	golf

Et ta famille? Et tes copains? pages 110–111

Ton père/Il/Ta sœur/Elle...	Does your father/he/your sister/she...
... aime faire du sport?	... like to do sport?
... aime sortir?	... like to go out?
... aime aller au...?	... like going to...?
Tes parents/Ils aiment... + inf.?	Do your parents/they like to...?
Tes sœurs/Elles aiment... + inf.?	Do your sisters/they like to...?
Ton frère/Il/Ta mère/Elle...	Does your brother/he/your mother/she...
... fait souvent du sport?	... often do sport?
... sort souvent?	... often go out?
... va souvent en ville?	... often go into town?
Tes copains/Ils...	Do your friends (boys, or boys and girls)/they...
Tes copines/Elles...	Do your friends (girls)/they
... font souvent du sport?	... do sport often?
... sortent souvent?	... go out often?
... vont souvent au...?	... go to ... often?

DiX sur DiX!

Can you ...
... say where you go when you go out and how often?
... ask others about the same?
... say what sports you play and ask others about what they play?
... say what your family like to do in their spare time and ask others?
... use more complex sentences?
... use verbs with *ils/elles* in the present tense?
... use *faire*, *aller* and *sortir* (singular + *ils/elles*)?
... remember more useful techniques for learning and working better?
... remember more about France?

Où est ma tortue?!?   pages 116–117

Où est le chat de Paul?	Where is Paul's cat?
Où est la tortue d'Emilie?	Where is Emilie's tortoise?
Il/Elle est…	It/He/She is…
dans…	in…
sur…	on…
sous…	under…
devant…	in front of…
derrière…	behind…
entre… et…	between… and…
le placard	the cupboard
le tiroir	the drawer
l'étagère	the shelf
la poubelle	the bin

Ton hamster dort souvent?   pages 118–119

Mon chien…	My dog…
mange (↔ manger)	eats (↔ to eat)
boit (↔ boire)	drinks (↔ to drink)
court (↔ courir)	runs (↔ to run)
dort (↔ dormir)	sleeps (↔ to sleep)
le matin	in the morning
à midi	at midday/at lunchtime
l'après-midi	in the afternoon
le soir	in the evening
la nuit	at night
Ton chat mange beaucoup?	Does your dog eat a lot?
Ton lapin dort quand?	When does your rabbit sleep?
Ta tortue aime manger?	Does your tortoise like to eat?

Nous jouons dans le jardin.	We play/We are playing in the garden.
Vous jouez	You play/You are playing
Nous regardons la télé.	We watch/We are watching TV.
Vous regardez	You watch/You are watching
Nous travaillons dans le garage.	We work/We are working in the garage.
Vous travaillez	You work/You are working
Nous allons au parc.	We go/We are going to the park.
Vous allez	You go/You are going
Nous faisons les courses.	We do/We are doing the shopping.
Vous faites	You do/You are doing
Nous avons musique.	We have/We are having music.
Vous avez	You have/You are having
Nous sommes fatigués.	We are tired.
Vous êtes fatigués.	You are tired.

Di✗ sur Di✗!

Can you …
- … say where things (or pets!) are and ask others where things are?
- … describe your pet's daily routine and ask others about theirs?
- … say what you and your pets do together and ask others about what they do?
- … use *de/d'* to indicate possession
- … use the present tense in full (regular -er verbs, as well as *avoir, être, faire* and *aller*)?
- … understand the difference between *on* and *nous*?
- … understand the difference between *tu* and *vous*?
- … remember more useful techniques for learning and working better?
- … remember more about France?

Mes animaux et moi

Tu vas où? pages 126–127

Tu vas où?/Vous allez où?	Where are you going?
samedi matin/après-midi/ soir	on Saturday morning/afternoon/ evening
ce matin/cet après-midi/ ce soir	this morning/this afternoon/ this evening
Je vais…	I am going…
Nous allons/On va…	We are going…
à la piscine	to the swimming pool
à la bibliothèque	to the library
à la cafétéria	to the cafeteria
aux magasins	to the shops
chez mes grands-parents	to my grandparents'

Nous allons au cinéma? pages 128–129

Il est quelle heure?	What time is it?
Il est midi (midi dix, etc.)	It's 12 o'clock/midday. (12.10, etc.)
Il est trois heures dix.	It is ten past three. (3.10)
Il est trois heures moins dix.	It is ten to three. (2.50).
Il est trois heures et quart.	It is quarter past three. (3.15)
Il est trois heures moins le quart.	It is quarter to three. (2.45)
Il est trois heures et demie.	It is half past three. (3.30)
Je sors/Tu sors	I go out/You go out
Il/Elle/On sort	He/She/One goes out
Nous sortons/Vous sortez	We go out/You go out
Ils/Elles sortent	They go out
Rendez-vous à quelle heure?	At what time shall we meet?
Rendez-vous à 4h20.	Let's meet at 4.20.
Rendez-vous où?	Where shall we meet?
Rendez-vous devant le cinéma.	Let's meet in front of the cinema/outside the cinema.

Paul, qu'est-ce que tu veux?	Paul, what do you want?
Je veux…	I want…
Je voudrais…	I would like…
un coca	one/a coca cola
un orangina	one/an orangina
une limonade	one/a lemonade
un milk-shake	one/a milk shake
un thé	one/a tea
un café	one/a coffee
un chocolat chaud	one/a hot chocolate
une glace au chocolat	one/a chocolate ice cream
une glace à la vanille	one/a vanilla ice cream
une glace à la fraise	one/a strawberry ice cream

DiX sur DiX!

Can you …
… say where you are going and when?
… ask others about the same?
… make arrangements with others for going out?
… make arrangements with others for meeting in town?
… say what drinks or ice-creams you want and ask others what they want?
… use *aller au/à la/aux/chez* accurately?
… use *sortir* in full in the present tense?
… remember more useful techniques for learning and working better?
… remember more about France?

J'adore sortir! 13

Mon père n'est pas très sportif   pages 136–137

Comment est ton beau-père?	What is your stepfather like?
Comment est ta belle-mère?	What is your stepmother like?
Il/Elle est...	He/She is...
strict, e	strict
patient, e	patient
sympathique	friendly
généreux, euse	generous
ennuyeux, euse	boring
travailleur, euse	hardworking
bricoleur, euse	keen on DIY
sportif, ive	sporty
un peu... (+ adjectif)	a little... (+ adjective)

Tu rentres à quelle heure?   pages 138–139

Je reste à la maison. (rester)	I am staying at home. (to stay)
Je vais en ville avec Julien.	I am going into town with Julien.
à pied	on foot/walking
en autobus	by bus
en vélo	by bicycle
en voiture	by car
avec Max et son père/	with Max and his father/
sa mère/ses parents	his mother/his parents
avec Anna et son père/	with Max and her father/
sa mère/ses parents	her mother/her parents
Tu pars à quelle heure?	At what time are you leaving?
(partir)	(to leave)
Je pars à...	I am leaving at...
Tu rentres à quelle heure?	At what time are you getting back?
Je rentre à...	I am getting back at...
(rentrer)	(to get back)

DiX sur DiX!

Can you …

… describe people's personalities and ask others?

… discuss going out and coming home?

… use some irregular adjectives in the feminine?

… use possessives *son/sa/ses* accurately?

… use *partir* in full in the present tense?

… remember more useful techniques for learning and working better?

… remember more about France?

a, ai, as	see avoir
à *prép*	to, at, in
activité *nf*	activity
adjectif *nm*	adjective
adverbe *nm*	adverb
adorer *v*	to adore
âge *nm*	age;
* tu as quel âge?	how old are you?
agrafeuse *nf*	stapler
aide *nm*	help;
* à l'aide de…	with the help of…
aider *v*	to help
aigü, e *adj*	-e- accent aigü = -é-
aimer *v*	to like; to love
allemand *nm*	German (*school subject*)
aller *v*	to go
alphabet *nm*	alphabet
amusant, e *adj*	funny
an *nm*	year;
* j'ai 11 ans	I am 11
anglais, e *adj*	English
anglais *nm*	English (*school subject*)
Angleterre *nf*	England
animal, -aux *nm*	animal; pet
anniversaire *nm*	birthday
août *nm*	August
appeler *v*	to call;
* je m'appelle	my name is
apprendre *v*	to learn
après-midi *nm/f*	afternoon
arrivée *nf*	arrival; finishing line
assez *adv*	fairly, quite
attention *nf* (also *excl*)	care; careful
au *prép*	to; to the; in
aujourd'hui *adv*	today
aussi *adv*	also, as well
autobus *nm*	bus
(*can be shortened to* bus)	
autorisé, e *adj*	allowed
avec *prép*	with
avoir *verb*	to have;
* j'ai 11 ans	I am 11
avril *nm*	April

babyfoot *nm*	table football
bande dessinée *nf*	cartoon strip
basket *nm*	basketball
bavard, e *adj*	talkative, chatty
BD	see **bande desinée**
beau-frère *nm*	stepbrother
beau-père *nm*	stepfather
beaucoup *adv*	much, a lot
belle-mère *nf*	stepmother
belle-sœur *nf*	stepsister
bête *adj*	silly, stupid
bibliothèque *nf*	library
bien *adv*	well, alright
bof *excl (fam)*	so so; well *(hesitation)*
boit *v*	see **boire**
boire *v*	to drink
bonjour *nm*	hello, good morning, good afternoon
bowling *nm*	ten pin bowling *(venue and game)*
bricoleur, -euse *adj*	keen on DIY
brosse *nf*	board duster
bruyant, e *adj*	loud, noisy
bulle *nf*	bubble; speech bubble
ça *pron*	this, that;
* ça va	it's alright, I'm alright
cacher *v*	to hide, to cover
cache-cache *nm*	hide-and-seek
cadeau *nm*	present
café *nm*	coffee
cafétéria *f*	cafeteria
cahier *nm*	exercise book
calculette *nf*	calculator
calme *adj*	calm, quiet
caractère *nm* * en caractères gras	in bold
carnet *nm*	notebook
carte *nf*	card; map
cassette *nf*	cassette
CD *nm*	CD
cédille *nf*	-c- cédille = -ç-
centre *nm*	centre
centre sportif *nm*	sports centre
commercial *nm*	shopping centre
centre-ville *nm*	town centre
chaise *nf*	chair
changer *v*	to change
changer de place *v*	move
chanson *nf*	song

chaque *adj*	each
chat *nm*	cat
chercher *v*	to look for; to look up
chien *nm*	dog
chocolat *nm*	chocolate
choisir *v*	to choose;
* choisis	choose (*instruction*)
choix *nm*	choice
cinéma *nm*	cinema
cinquante *num*	fifty
circonflexe *adj*	-e- accent circonflexe = -ê-
classe *nf*	class; classroom
classer *v*	to classify
club *nm*	club
club des jeunes *nm*	youth club
cobaye *nm*	guinea pig
coca *nm*	Coke (R)
cocher *v*	to tick
cœur *nm*	heart;
* par cœur	by heart
collège *nm*	secondary school (11–15)
colonne *nf*	column
commencer *v*	to start
comment *adv*	how;
* comment?	pardon?;
tu t'appelles comment?	what's your name?;
ça s'écrit comment?	how is it spelt?
il est comment?	what is he like?
commercial *adj*	commercial
compléter *v*	to complete
comprendre *v*	to understand
console vidéo *nf*	games console
continuer *v*	to continue
copain *nm*	friend (*male*)
copine *nf*	friend (*female*)
correctement *adv*	correctly
correspondre *v*	to correspond;
* fais correspondre	match up (*instruction*)
corriger *v*	to correct
courir *v*	to run
courses *nfpl*	shopping;
* faire les courses	to do the shopping
court *v*	see **courir**
craie *nf*	chalk; piece of chalk
crayon *nm*	pencil
cricket *nm*	cricket (*sport*)

d'accord *excl*	OK
dans *prép*	in
danse *nf*	dancing
date *nf*	date
dé *nm*	dice
décembre *nm*	December
décorer *v*	to decorate
découper *v*	to cut
décrire *v*	to describe
déjeuner *nm*	lunch
demi, e *adj*	half;
* … et demi(e)	half past…
demi-frère *nm*	half-brother
demi-sœur *nf*	half-sister
derrière *prép*	behind
des *art*	some
désolé, e *adj*	sorry
dessin *nm*	drawing, picture; art (*school subject*)
dessiner *v*	to draw
deux *num*	two;
* à deux	in pairs
devant *prép*	in front of
deviner *v*	to guess
devoirs *nmpl*	homework
dialogue *nm*	dialogue
dictionnaire *nm*	dictionary
difficile *adj*	difficult, hard
dimanche *nm*	Sunday
dire *v*	to say
dis	see dire
discuter *v*	to discuss
dix *num*	ten
doigt *nm*	finger;
* lève le doigt	raise your hand (*instruction*)
donner *v*	to give
dormir *v*	to sleep
dort *v*	see dormir
double *adj*	double -v- = -w-
drôle *adj*	funny
échanger *v*	to swap
Ecosse *nf*	Scotland
écouter *v*	to listen, to listen to
écran *nm*	screen
écrire *v*	to write;
* ça s'écrit comment?	how is it spelt?;
écris	write (*instruction*)

écrit *adj*	written;
* par écrit	in writing
éducation *nf*	education
éducation civique et sociale *nf*	PSE
éducation religieuse *nf*	RE
église *nf*	church
élégant, e *adj*	smart, elegant
elle *pron*	she; it
embêtant, e *adj*	annoying
ennuyeux, -euse *adj*	boring
entre *prép*	between
erreur *nf*	error, mistake
es, est	see **être**
espagnol *nm*	Spanish (*school subject*)
et *conj*	and
étagère *nf*	shelf
étiquette *nf*	label
être *v*	to be
exact, e *adj*	exact; correct
exemple *nm*	example
exercice *nm*	exercise
exploiter *v*	to use
exposé *nm*	presentation (*oral*)
expression *nf*	phrase
facile *adj*	easy
faire *v*	to do; to make
faire correspondre *v*	to match up
faire les courses *v*	to do the shopping
fais	see **faire**
famille *nf*	family
fatigant, e *adj*	tiring
fatigué, e *adj*	tired
faux, -ausse *adj*	false, wrong
féminin *adj*	feminine
fenêtre *nf*	window
fermer *v*	to close
féroce *adj*	fierce
festivité *fpl*	festivities
feuille *nf*	sheet of paper; worksheet
feutre *nm*	felt-tip pen
février *nm*	February
fille *nf*	girl, daughter
fille unique *nf*	only child (*girl*)
fils *nm*	son
fils unique *nf*	only child (*boy*)
finir *v*	to finish

fleur *nf*	flower
font *v*	see **faire**
football *nm*	football
formule *nf*	formula
fraise *nf*	strawberry
français, e *adj*	French
français *nm*	French (*school subject*)
France *nf*	France
frère *nm*	brother
gagner *v*	to win
garage *nm*	garage
généreux, -euse *adj*	generous
géographie *nf*	geography (*sometimes* géo)
gerbille *nf*	gerbil
geste *nm*	gesture
glace *nf*	ice cream
glossaire *nm*	glossary
golf *nm*	golf
gomme *nf*	rubber
grammaire *nf*	grammaire
grand, e *adj*	tall
grand-parent *nm*	grandparent
gras *adj* * en caractères gras	in bold
grave *adj*	-e- accent grave = -è-
grec *adj*	-i- grec = -y-
grille *nf*	grid
groupe *nm*	group
habiter *v*	to live
hamster *nm*	hamster
haut, e *adj*	high;
* à haute voix	aloud
heure *nf*	hour; time;
* deux heures	two o'clock
histoire *nf*	history (subject); story
hockey *nm*	hockey
idéal, e *adj*	ideal
il *pron*	he; it;
* il y a	there is, there are
illustrer *v*	to illustrate
imiter *v*	to imitate
improviser *v*	to improvise
indiqué, e *adj*	indicated
infinitif *nm*	infinitive
info, information *nf*	information; news
informatique *nf*	IT, computer studies
intelligent, e *adj*	intelligent, clever

intéressant, e *adj*	interesting
Internet *nm*	Internet
intrus *nm*	odd one out
inventer *v*	to invent, to make up
inviter *v*	to invite
Irlande *nf*	Ireland
Irlande du Nord *nf*	Northern Ireland
janvier *nm*	January
je *pron*	I
jeu, x *nm*	game
jeudi *nm*	Thursday
jouer *v*	to play; to act out
joueur, -euse *nm/f*	player
juillet *nm*	July
juin *nm*	June
la *art*	the (*f*)
lapin *nm*	rabbit
le *art*	the (*m*)
leçon *nf*	learning homework
lecture *nf*	reading
lent, e *adj*	slow
les *art*	the (*pl*)
lettre *nf*	letter
ligne *nf*	line
limonade *nf*	lemonade
lire *v*	to read;
* lis/lisez	read (*instruction*)
livre *nm*	book; textbook
loto *nm*	bingo
lundi *nm*	Monday
ma *adj*	my
madame *nf*	Mrs, madam
mademoiselle *nf*	Miss
magasin *nm*	shop
magnétophone *nm*	cassette player
mai *nm*	May
mais *conj*	but
maison *nf*	house;
* à la maison	at home
manger *v*	to eat
mardi *nm*	Tuesday
marqueur *nm*	marker pen
mars *nm*	March
masculin *adj*	masculine
maths *nfpl*	maths
matière *nf*	school subject

matin *nm*	morning
mémoire *nf*	memory;
* de mémoire	from memory
mémoriser *v*	to learn by heart
merci *excl*	thank you
mercredi *nm*	Wednesday
mère *nf*	mother
mes *adj*	my
milk-shake *nm*	milk shake
modèle *nm*	model
moi *pron*	me;
* à moi	mine, my turn
mois *nm*	month
moins *adv, prép*	less; minus
mon *adj*	my
monsieur *nm*	Mr, sir
montrer *v*	to show; to point to
mot *nm*	word
musique *nf*	music
nom *nm*	name; noun
nombre *nm*	number
non *adv*	no
nous *pron*	we; us
novembre *nm*	November
nuit *nf*	night
nul *adv (fam)*	awful, useless
numéro *nm*	number
octobre *nm*	October
œuf *nm*	egg
offrir *v*	to give (*as a present*)
oiseau, x *nm*	bird
on *pron*	one, we, they (= *people in general*);
	we (= *we ourselves*)
ont *v*	see avoir
oral *adj*	oral
oralement *adv*	orally
orangina *nm*	Orangina (R)
ordinateur *nm*	computer
ordre *nm*	order;
* dans l'ordre	in the correct order
ou *conj*	or
où *adv*	where
oublier *v*	to forget
oui *adv*	yes
ouvrir *v*	to open
page *nf*	page

paire *nf*	pair
Pâques *nfpl*	Easter
paragraphe *nm*	paragraph
parc *nm*	park
parce que *conj*	because
parent *nm*	parent
pars, part *v*	see partir
partenaire *nm/f*	partner
partir *v*	to leave, to set off
pas *adv*	not;
* pas du tout	not at all
patient, e *adj*	patient
patinoire *nf*	ice rink
pays de Galles *nm*	Wales
peluche *nf*	soft toy
père *nm*	father
personnel *adj*	personal
petit, e *adj*	small
peu *adv* un peu	a little
peux, peut *v*	see pouvoir
photo *nf*	photo
phrase *nf*	sentence
pied *nm*	foot;
* à pied	on foot
piscine *nf*	swimming pool
placard *nm*	cupboard
plaisir *nm*	pleasure
plaît, s'il te plaît/s'il vous plaît	please
platine laser *nf*	CD player
pluriel *adj*	plural
plus *adv, prép*	more; plus
poème *nm*	poem
point *nm*	point
poisson *nm*	fish
ponctuation *nf*	punctuation
porte *nf*	door
poser une question *v*	to ask a question
poster *nm*	poster
poubelle *nf*	bin
pourquoi *adv*	why
pratiquer *v*	to practise
préférer *v*	to prefer;
* je préfère	I prefer
premier *adj*	first
prendre *v*	to take
prénom *nm*	first name

préparer *v*	to prepare
problème *nm*	problem
professeur *nm*	teacher (*also:* le/la prof)
qu'	see que
quand *adv*	when
quarante *num*	forty
quart *nm*	quarter;
* … et quart	quarter past;
… moins le quart	quarter to…
que *conj*	what;
* qu'est-ce que …?	what is …?
quel, quelle *adj*	which;
* à quelle heure?	at what time?
quelquefois *adv*	sometimes
question *nf*	question
qui *pron*	who;
* c'est à qui?	whose turn is it?
raison *nf*	reason
rap *nm*	rap
rapide *adj*	fast
rarement *adv*	rarely
réalité *nf*	reality
recommencer *v*	to start again
recopier *v*	to copy out
réécouter *v*	to listen again
regarder *v*	to look at, to watch
règle *nf*	ruler
relire *v*	to read again;
* relis	read again (*instruction*)
remplacer *v*	to replace
rendez-vous *nm*	meeting, date;
* rendez-vous dans le parc	let's meet in the park
rentrer *v*	to get back
répéter *v*	to repeat
répondre *v*	to answer
réponse *nf*	answer
rester *v*	to stay
résultat *nm*	result
revoir *nm* au revoir	good bye
rôle *nm*	role, part;
* change de rôle	change part;
à tour de rôle	in turn
rugby *nm*	rugby
sa *adj*	his; her; its
sac *nm*	bag
sais	see savoir

salle *nf*	room (*in school, not in house*)
salut *excl* (*fam*)	hello; hi; goodbye
samedi *nm*	Saturday
sans *prép*	without
savoir	to know
sciences *nfpl*	science
septembre *nm*	September
ses *adj*	his; her; its
seul, e *adj*	alone
singulier *adj*	singular
sketch *nm*	sketch
sœur *nf*	sister
soir *nm*	evening
soixante *num*	sixty
son *adj*	his; her; its
sont *v*	see être
sors, sort *v*	see sortir
sortir *v*	to go out
souligner *v*	to underline
souris *nf*	mouse
sous *prép*	under
souvent *adv*	often
sport *nm*	sport, PE, games
sportif, -ve *adj*	sporty
strict, e *adj*	strict
stylo *nm*	pen, biro
stylo-plume *nm*	fountain pen
suis *v*	see être
sur *prep*	on; about
surfer *v*	to surf;
* surfer sur Internet	to surf the Internet
sympathique *adj*	friendly (*can be shortened to* sympa)
ta *adj*	your
table *nf*	table; desk
tableau *nm*	board (*in the classroom*)
technologie *nf* (*or* techno)	design and technology (D&T)
télévision *nf* (*sometimes* télé)	television
tennis *nm*	tennis
tes *adj*	your
texte *nm*	text
thé *nm*	tea
thème *nm*	topic
timide *adj*	shy
tiroir *nm*	drawer
toi *pron*	you;
* avec toi	with you;

à toi	yours, your turn
toilettes *nfpl*	toilets
ton *adj*	your
tortue *nf*	tortoise
tout *adj*	all;
* pas du tout	not at all
traduire *v*	to translate
travail *nm*	work
travailler *v*	to work
travailleur, -euse *adj*	hardworking
trente *num*	thirty
très *adv*	very
trombone *nm*	paper clip
trop *adv*	too, too much
trousse *nf*	pencil case
trouver *v*	to find
tu *pron*	you *ms*
un, une *art*	a; one
uniquement *adv*	only
utiliser *v*	to use
va, vais, va	see **aller**;
* ça va	it's alright; I'm alright
vanille *nf*	vanilla
vélo *nm*	bicycle
vendredi *nm*	Friday
verbe *nm*	verb
vérifier *v*	to check
vêtements *nmpl*	clothes
veux *v*	want (*from infinitive* **vouloir**, to want)
ville *nf*	town
vingt *num*	twenty
vite *adv*	quickly
vocabulaire *nm*	vocabulary
voilà *prép*	here is; here you are
voiture *nm*	car
voix *nf*	voice;
* à haute voix	aloud
volley-ball *nm*	volleyball
vont *v*	see **aller**
voudrais	would like (*from infinitive* **vouloir**, to want)
vouloir	to want
vous *pron*	you
vrai, e *nf*	true
yeux *nmpl*	eyes

a *art*	un; une
adjective *n*	adjectif *f*
adore *v*	adorer
adverb *n*	adverbe *m*
afternoon *n*	après-midi *m/f*
alone *adj*	seul, e
alright *adj/adv*	bien
also *adv*	aussi
and *conj*	et
animal *n*	animal *m*
annoying *adj*	embêtant, e
answer *n*	réponse *f*
April *n*	avril *m*
art (*school subject*) *n*	dessin *m*
at *prep*	(see Les prépositions, *AnneXe* p 56–57)
August *n*	août *m*
awful *adj*	nul, le
basketball *n*	basket *m*
be *v*	être
be able to *v*	pouvoir
because *conj*	parce que; parce qu' (before word beginning with a vowel)
behind *prep*	derrière
between *adv*	entre
bicycle *n*	vélo *m*
bin *n*	poubelle *f*
bird *n*	oiseau, x *m*
birthday *n*	anniversaire *m*
board *n*	tableau *m*
board duster *n*	brosse *f*
book *n*	livre *m*
boring *adj*	ennuyeux, -euse
brother *n*	frère *m*
bus *n*	autobus *m*
but *prep*	mais
cafeteria *n*	cafétéria *f*
calm *adj*	calme
can *v*	pouvoir
car *n*	voiture *f*
cassette *n*	cassette *f*
cassette player *n*	magnétophone *m*
cat *n*	chat *m*

CD *n*	CD *m*
CD player *n*	platine laser *f*
chair *n*	chaise *f*
chalk (piece of) *n*	craie *f*
chatty *adj*	bavard, e
chocolate *n*	chocolat *m*
church *n*	église *f*
cinema *n*	cinéma *m*
classroom *n*	salle *f*
close *v*	fermer
clothes *n*	vêtements *mpl*
club *n*	club *m*
coffee *n*	café *m*
Coke (R) *n*	coca *m*
computer *m*	ordinateur *m*
computer studies *n*	informatique *f*
correct *v*	corriger
cricket *n*	cricket *m*
cupboard *n*	placard *m*
dancing *n*	danse *f*
date *n*	date *f*
December *n*	décembre *m*
decorate *v*	décorer
desk *n*	table *f*
design and technology (*or D&T*)	technologie *f*
dictionary *n*	dictionnaire *m*
difficult *adj*	difficile
DIY	*see* keen
do *v*	faire;
* to do the shopping	faire les courses
dog *n*	chien *m*
door *n*	porte *f*
draw *v*	dessiner
drawer *n*	tiroir *m*
drawing *n*	dessin *m*
drink *v*	boire
D&T (*or design* and *technology*) *n*	technologie *f*
Easter *n*	Pâques *fpl*
easy *adj*	facile
eat *v*	manger
egg *n*	œuf *m*
elegant *adj*	élégant, e
English *adj*	anglais, e
English *n*	anglais *m*
evening *n*	soir *m*
exercise book *n*	cahier *m*

fairly *adv*	assez
family *n*	famille *f*
fast *adj*	rapide
father *n*	père *m*
February *n*	février *m*
feminine *adj*	féminin, e
fierce *adj*	féroce
fifty *num*	cinquante
first *adj*	premier, ère
fish *n*	poisson *m*
foot *n* * on foot	à pied
football *n*	football *m*
forty *num*	quarante
France *n*	France *f*
French (*school subject*) *n*	français *m*
Friday *n*	vendredi *m*
friend *n*	copain *m*; copine *f*
friendly *adj*	sympa; sympathique
front, in front of *prep*	devant
funny *adj*	amusant, drôle
game *n*	jeu *m*
games (*sports*) *npl*	sport *m*
games console *n*	console vidéo *f*
garage *n*	garage *m*
generous *adj*	généreux, -euse
geography *n*	géographie *f*
gerbil *n*	gerbille *f*
German *n*	allemand *m*
get back *v*	rentrer
give *n*	donner; (*as a present*) offrir
go *v*	aller
go out	sortir
goodbye *excl*	au revoir; salut (*fam*)
golf *n*	golf *m*
grandparent *n*	grand-parent *m*
guinea pig *n*	cobaye *m*
half *adj*	demi, e
* half past	… et demie
hamster *n*	hamster *m*
hardworking *adj*	travailleur, -euse
have *v*	avoir
he *pron*	il
hello *excl*	bonjour; salut (*fam*)
help *v*	aider
her *adj*	son; sa; ses
here, here is/here are *adv*	voilà

his *adj*	son; sa; ses
history *n*	histoire *f*
hockey *n*	hockey *m*
home *n*	maison *f;*
* at home	à la maison
homework *n*	devoirs *mpl*
house *n*	maison *f*
how *adv*	comment
I *pron*	je; j'
ice cream *n*	glace *f*
ideal *adj*	idéal, e
in *prep*	(see Les prépositions, *AnneXe* p 56–57)
intelligent *adj*	intelligent, e
Internet *n*	Internet *m*
invite *v*	inviter
Ireland *n*	Irlande *f;*
Northern Ireland	Irlande du Nord *f*
it *pron*	il; elle
IT (= ICT) *n*	informatique *f*
its *pron*	son; sa; ses
January *n*	janvier *m*
July *n*	juillet *n*
June *n*	juin *m*
keen on DIY *adj*	bricoleur, -euse *adj*
know *v*	savoir;
* I know	je sais
learn *v*	apprendre
leave *v*	partir
lemonade *n*	limonade *f*
less *adv*	moins
library *n*	bibliothèque *f*
like *v*	aimer;
* I would like	je voudrais
listen (to) *v*	écouter
little *adj*	petit, e;
a little	un peu
live *v*	habiter
look (at) *v*	regarder
lot, a lot *adv*	beaucoup
lunch *n*	déjeuner *m*
make *v*	faire
March *n*	mars *m*
masculine *adj*	masculin, e
maths *n*	maths *fpl*
May *n*	mai *m*

anglais–français

me *pron*	moi
meet *v,* let's meet…	rendez-vous…
milk shake *n*	milk-shake *m*
mine *pron*	à moi
minus *prep*	moins
Miss *n*	mademoiselle *f*
Monday *n*	lundi *m*
more *adv*	plus
morning *n*	matin *m*
mother *n*	mère *f*
mouse *n*	souris *f*
move *v*	changer de place
Mr *n*	monsieur *m*
Mrs *n*	madame *f*
much *adv*	beaucoup
music *n*	musique *f*
my *adj*	mon, ma, mes;
* it's my turn	c'est à moi
name *n*	nom *m*;
* my name is	je m'appelle
night *n*	nuit *f*
no *excl*	non
noisy *adj*	bruyant, e
not *adv*	pas;
* not at all	pas du tout
notebook *n*	carnet *m*
November *n*	novembre *m*
o'clock *adv*	… heures;
* two o'clock	deux heures
October *n*	octobre *m*
often *adv*	souvent
OK *excl*	d'accord
old, how old are you? *adj*	tu as quel âge?
on *prep*	sur
one *num*	un, une
only child (*boy*)	fils unique *m*
only child (*girl*)	fille unique *f*
open *v*	ouvrir
or *prep*	ou
Orangina (R) *n*	orangina *m*
parent *n*	parent *m*
park *n*	parc *m*
patient *adj*	patient, e
PE *n*	sport *m*
pen *n*	stylo *m*
pencil *n*	crayon *m*

pet *n*	animal (à la maison) *m*
play *v*	jouer
please *excl*	s'il te plaît; s'il vous plaît
plural *adj*	pluriel
plus *prep*	plus
poem *n*	poème *m*
poster *n*	poster *m*
practise *v*	pratiquer
prefer *v*	préférer (je préfère)
present *n*	cadeau *m*
PSE *n*	éducation civique et sociale *f*
quarter *n*	quart *m*;
* quarter past…	… et quart;
quarter to…	… moins le quart
quickly *adv*	vite
quiet *adj*	calme
quite *adv*	assez
rabbit *n*	lapin *m*
rarely *adv*	rarement
rap *n*	rap *m*
RE *n*	éducation religieuse *f*
read *v*	lire
reading *n*	lecture *f*
return *v*	rentrer
room (*classroom*) *n*	salle *f*
rubber *n*	gomme *f*
rugby *n*	rugby *m*
ruler *n*	règle *f*
run *v*	courir
Saturday *n*	samedi *m*
school (secondary)	collège *m*
science *n*	sciences *nfpl*
Scotland *n*	Ecosse *f*
screen *n*	écran *m*
September *n*	septembre *m*
she *pron*	elle
sheet of paper *n*	feuille *f*
shelf *n*	étagère *f*
shy *adj*	timide
shop *n*	magasin *m*
shopping centre	centre commercial *m*
singular *adj*	singulier
sir *n*	monsieur *m*
sister *n*	sœur *f*
sixty *num*	soixante
sleep *v*	dormir

slow *adj*	lent, e
small *adj*	petit, e
soft toy	peluche *f*
sometimes *adv*	quelquefois
song *n*	chanson *f*
sorry *adj*	désolé, e
so so *adv*	bof
Spanish (*school subject*) *n*	espagnol *m*
sport *n*	sport *m*
sports centre *n*	centre sportif *m*
sporty *adj*	sportif, -ive
start *v*	commencer
stay *v*	rester
stepbrother *n*	beau-frère *m*
stepfather *n*	beau-père *m*
stepmother *m*	belle-mère *f*
stepsister *n*	belle-sœur *f*
strawberry *n*	fraise *f*
strict *adj*	strict, e
stupid *adj*	bête
Sunday *n*	dimanche *m*
surf *v*	surfer
swimming pool *n*	piscine *f*
table *n*	table *nf*
table football *n*	babyfoot *m*
talkative *adj*	bavard, e
tall *adj*	grand, e
tea *n*	thé *m*
television *n*	télévision (*sometimes* télé) *f*
ten *num*	dix;
ten pin bowling *n*	bowling *m*
tennis *n*	tennis *m*
textbook *n*	livre *m*
thank you *excl*	merci
that; I like that *pron*	ça; j'aime ça
the *art*	le; la; l'; les
thirty *num*	trente
Thursday *n*	jeudi *m*
tired *adj*	fatigué, e
tiring *adj*	fatigant, e
to *prep*	(see Les prépositions, *AnneXe* p 56–57)
today *adv*	aujourd'hui
toilets *n*	toilettes *nfpl*
too *adv*	trop
tortoise *n*	tortue *f*

town *n*	ville *f*
town centre *n*	centre-ville *m*
toy *n*	jouet *m*
Tuesday *n*	mardi *m*
twenty *num*	vingt
two *num*	deux
under *prep*	sous
us *pron*	nous
useless *adj*	nul, le
vanilla *n*	vanille *f*
video game *n*	jeu vidéo *m*
very *adv*	très
volleyball *n*	volley-ball *m*
Wales *n*	pays de Galles *m*
want *v*	vouloir
watch *v*	regarder
we *pron*	nous; on
Wednesday *n*	mercredi *m*
well *adv*	bien
what *pron*	qu'est-ce que;
* what's your name?	tu t'appelles comment?;
what is he like?	il est comment?
when *adv*	quand
where *adv*	où
which *adj*	quel, le
who *pron*	qui
whose *pron*	c'est à qui?
why *adv*	pourquoi
window *n*	fenêtre *f*
with *prep*	avec
without *prep*	sans
work *n*	travail *m*
work *v*	travailler
worksheet *n*	feuille *f*
write *v*	écrire
year *n*	an *m*;
* I'm 11 years old	j'ai 11 ans
yes *excl*	oui
you *pron*	tu; toi;
* with you	avec toi
your *adj*	ton; ta; tes
* it's your turn	c'est à toi
youth club *n*	club des jeunes *m*

Les noms (n) – Nouns

◄◄ to Formule X pp27, 28, 57

Nouns can be people (*mon père*), animals (*un chat*), objects (*une règle*) or places (*un parc*).

Masculine and feminine

● In French, every noun has a gender, and is either masculine (*m*) or feminine (*f*). You can rarely guess which, so every time you learn a new noun you must learn its gender too.

● You will usually find *le* (or *l'* before nouns beginning with a vowel), *les, un, des, mon, ton,* and *son* before masculine nouns:
l'oiseau the bird
un livre a book
ton frère your brother

● You will usually find *la* (or *l'* before nouns beginning with a vowel), *les, une, des, ma, ta,* and *sa* before feminine nouns:
la tortue the tortoise
une chaise a chair
mes sœurs my sisters

Singular and plural

● Most nouns can be used either in the singular (*s*) or in the plural (*pl*).

● To indicate a plural, you normally add an –s to the end of the noun:
un chat a cat   *deux chats* two cats
ma copine my friend   *mes copines* my friends

There are some exceptions, though. For example:

Nouns ending in *-al* and in *-au* in the singular end with *-aux* in the plural:
un animal   *des animaux*
un oiseau   *des oiseaux*

Nouns ending in *-s* already stay the same in the plural:
une souris   *des souris*

● The *-s* of the plural is silent, and so *chat* sounds like *chats*, and *copines* sounds like *copine*.

Articles are short words that are used before nouns.

The = *le, la, l'* or *les*
le + masculine singular noun	*le lapin*	the rabbit
la + feminine singular noun	*la feuille*	the sheet
l' before a vowel	*l'oiseau*	the bird
les + plural noun (masculine or feminine)	*les chiens*	the dogs

A, an (*pl* some) = *un, une* (*pl* des)
un + masculine singular noun	*un lapin*	a rabbit
une + feminine singular noun	*une feuille*	a sheet
des + plural noun (masculine or feminine)	*des chiens*	dogs, some dogs

Negatives: de or d'

In negative sentences, the articles *un, une* and *des* become *de* (or *d'* before a vowel):
J'ai un livre. I have a book. → *Je n'ai pas de livre.* I don't have a book.
Il a des animaux. He has pets. → *Il n'a pas d'animaux.* He doesn't have pets.

Other uses for articles

- *Le, la, l'* and *les* are also used when giving opinions in French. (This is different from English, which doesn't use articles in this type of phrase). For example:
  Tu aimes la musique? Do you like music?
  J'adore les animaux. I adore animals.
  Le bowling, c'est super! Ten-pin bowling is great!

- The article *le* is also used when talking about the day of the week or the date, such as:
  Aujourd'hui, c'est le 14 juin. Today is 14th June.
  J'ai maths le mardi. I have maths on Tuesdays.

La possession – Possession
◄◄ to Formule X pp39, 60, 63, 117, 139, 142

Mon, ma, mes, etc.

Words like *mon*, *ma*, *mes* are called possessive adjectives (*des adjectifs possessifs*).

'My' can translate as *mon*, *ma* or *mes*.
'Your' can translate as *ton*, *ta*, or *tes*.
'His', 'her' and 'its' can translate as *son*, *sa* or *ses*.

To decide which possessive adjective to use in French, look carefully at the noun which follows:
– if the noun is masculine singular, you need to use *mon/ton/son*
– if the noun is feminine singular, you need to use *ma/ta/sa*
– if the noun is plural (masculine <u>or</u> feminine), you need to use *mes/tes/ses*.

Example
*J'ai **ma** règle, mais où est **mon** stylo?*
I've got my ruler, but where is my pen?

Using de/d'

To indicate possession in English, we use *'s* at the end of a word. To show this in French, use *de* (or *d'* before a vowel), and watch the word order carefully. For example:
*C'est le livre **de** Magalie.*
It's Magalie**'s** book [↔ It is the book of Magalie].

Les adjectifs (adj) – Adjectives
◄◄ to Formule X pp59, 79, 137, 142

Introduction

Adjectives are words that describe nouns.

● In English, the spelling of an adjective does not depend on the thing or things it describes:
My father is *funny*.
My sister is *funny*.
My dogs are *funny*.

- In French, on the other hand, most adjectives can have two, three or four different spellings, depending on what or who they describe:
  Mon père est amusant.
  Ma sœur est amusante.
  Mes chiens sont amusants.

- When using adjectives, the word order in sentences isn't always the same in French as it is in English: there is more on this in *Formule X* Book 2.

- Dictionaries usually show adjectives in the masculine singular.

The feminine of adjectives

- Most adjectives (or 'regular' adjectives) add an *-e* at the end in the feminine:
  Mon père est petit. My father is small.
  Ma mère est petite. My mother is small.

- Adjectives which end anyway in *-e* stay the same in the feminine:
  Mon chat est timide. My cat is shy.
  Ma tortue est timide. My tortoise is shy.

- Some adjectives ('irregular' adjectives) follow different patterns:
  généreux → *généreuse* (generous)
  ennuyeux → *ennuyeuse* (boring)
  bricoleur → *bricoleuse* (keen on DIY)
  travailleur → *travailleuse* (hardworking)
  sportif → *sportive* (sporty)

- There are many different ways to show feminine endings in dictionaries. Some dictionaries show regular feminine endings like this: petit, e. They show other feminine endings like this: ennuyeux, -euse.

The plural of adjectives

- Most adjectives take an *-s* in the plural:
  John est sportif. John is sporty.
  Mes copains sont sportifs. My friends are sporty.

- You will learn more about the plural of adjectives in *Formule X* Book 2.

Les adverbes (adv) – Adverbs

◄◄ *to Formule X p41*

- Adverbs are words or phrases that tell you more about a verb or an adjective.

- They are invariable, which means they are always spelt in the same way, whatever they describe.

rarement rarely	*très* very
plus more	*quelquefois* sometimes
beaucoup a lot, much	*moins* less
souvent often	*trop* too, too much
ne ... pas not/don't/doesn't	*un peu* a little
bien well	*ne ... pas du tout* not at all
assez fairly	

Examples:

*Tu es **très** fatigant!* You are very tiring!

*L'histoire, c'est **assez** difficile.* History is fairly difficult.

- In English, adverbs can come either before or after a verb. For example:

I rarely play.　　　　　He works well.

In French, however, adverbs come after the verb:

*Je joue **rarement**.* I rarely play.

*Il travaille **bien**.* He works well.

Be careful with sentences using *ne* (or *n'*), though:

*Je **ne** joue **pas** du tout.* I don't play at all.

Les prépositions (prép) – Prepositions

◄◄ *to Formule X pp22, 98, 126, 132*

- Prepositions are words like 'in', 'on' and 'with', which show how one thing (or person, animal, idea) is related to another.

- In English, prepositions can have several meanings, depending on their context. For example, 'under', in 'The cat is under the chair' isn't the same as in 'She is under a lot of stress'. The same thing happens in French. This is why a preposition like 'in' has several possible translations in French.

Prepositions to/in/at → en/au/à/à la/aux/dans/chez

- Countries: use *au* with masculine countries and *en* with feminine countries. All the countries you have learnt so far are feminine except for one (Wales):

I live in Ireland. *J'habite **en** Irlande.*
I live in Wales. *J'habite **au** Pays de Galles.*

- Towns: use *à* when saying or asking which town someone lives in.
  Do you live in Toulouse? *Tu habites **à** Toulouse?*

- Other places (movement):
  I go to the park. *Je vais **au** parc.* (because *parc* is masculine singular)
  She goes to the swimming pool. *Il va **à la** piscine.* (*piscine* is feminine singular)
  We go to (the) church. *On va **à l'**église.* (*église* is singular and begins with a vowel)
  She goes to the shops. *Elle va **aux** magasins.* (*magasins* is plural. Use *aux* with both masculine <u>and</u> feminine nouns)

- Other places (no movement):
  My dog is in the park. *Mon chien est **dans** le parc.*
  We are in the garage. *Nous sommes **dans** le garage.*

- Someone's home (…'s):
  I am going to Julie's. *Je vais **chez** Julie.*
  I am at my brother's. *Je suis **chez** mon frère.*

- Infinitives
  In English, the infinitive of a verb will have the word 'to' in front of it (for example, 'to play', 'to work' and so on). If you want to translate an English infinitive into French, however, you don't need to translate the 'to'. The French infinitive does it for you! For example:
  to play *jouer*   He wants to play. *Il veut jouer.*

Other useful examples

at 3.00 *à 3h00*   on Mondays *le lundi*
iin the morning *le matin*   in the book *dans le livre*
in room 24 *en salle 24*
They go to/into town *Ils vont en ville* (but: *Ils vont au centre-ville*)
I play Scrabble *Je joue **au** Scrabble*
I play tennis *Je joue **au** tennis*
a chocolate ice cream (strawberry…) *une glace **au** chocolat (… **à la** fraise)*

Other prepositions

sur on	*sous* under	*entre* between
avec with	*devant* in front of	*derrière* behind

Verbs tell you what their subjects are doing (or did, will do, etc.) or being:

My brother went to Alton Towers. (subject = 'my brother')

He felt sick. (subject = 'he')

The infinitive

- When you look up a verb in a dictionary, the infinitive is the form you will usually find. French infinitives can end in *-er*, *-ir* or *-re*:

  dessiner to draw   *sortir* to go out   *lire* to read

- When two verbs are used in a row, the second one appears in the infinitive:

  *Elle préfère **sortir.*** She prefers to go out.

  *Je veux **dormir.*** I want to sleep.

Verb agreements

- Unless they are used in the infinitive (see above), French verbs change their spelling depending on their subject:

  J'écoute I listen   *Tu écoutes* You listen

  Les chiens écoutent The dogs listen

Tenses

- Verbs also change depending on what tense you use. In *Formule X* Book 1, we concentrate on the present tense.

Pronouns for use before verbs

Singular

je = I   Use *j'* instead before verbs that begin with a vowel (or some verbs beginning with *h*). Unlike the English 'I', *je* (or *j'*) only starts with a capital letter when it is the first word in a new sentence.

je joue I play   *j'ai* I have   *j'habite* I live

tu = you   Use *tu* when addressing <u>one</u> friend or relative, or a young person your age (or your cat, your dog, etc.!):

tu travailles you work

il = he; it   Useful to avoid repetition of a masculine noun:

il lit he reads (↔ *Paul lit* Paul reads; *mon frère lit* my brother reads)

elle = she; it — Useful to avoid repetition of a feminine noun:
elle mange she/it eats (↔ *la souris mange* the mouse eats)

on = they; one — Used for 'they' ('one' is a bit old-fashioned) when referring to people in general:
En Belgique, on parle français
In Belgium, they speak French
Also often used for 'we', instead of *nous* in speaking or informal writing:
on va souvent au cinéma
we often go to the cinema

Plural

nous = we — Can be used any time to translate 'we'. Better than *on* in formal writing.
nous sommes fatigués we are tired

vous = you — Used when addressing several people:
Max, Sophie, vous travaillez?
Max, Sophie, are you working?

ils = they — Useful to avoid repetition of a masculine noun:
Mes copains? Ils sont en ville.
My friends? They are in town.

elles = they — Useful to avoid repetition of a feminine noun:
J'ai deux tortues: elles sont drôles.
I have two tortoises: they are funny.

Notes

– When you use a verb with *on*, use the same form of the verb that you would use with *il* and *elle*, even though *on* refers to more than one person.
– Next year, you will learn that *vous* is also used instead of *tu* when addressing one person who is not a friend, a relative or a young person your age. It is considered more polite.
– Verb endings with *il* are the same as, say, with *Paul* or with *mon frère*, because the idea is the same:
Paul travaille. Paul works.
Mon frère travaille. My brother works.
Il travaille. He works.

The same goes for *elle* (↔ *Sophie; ma copine;* etc.), and for *ils* and *elles* (↔ *Max et Sophie; mes animaux;* etc.).

– When you need to translate 'they' into French, and you are talking about a combination of masculine and feminine nouns (to describe a group of girls and boys, or different animals, for example), use *ils*:
Mon chien et ma tortue? Ils sont dans le jardin.
My dog and my tortoise? They are in the garden.

The present tense

● The present tense is used to describe what is happening now, or what happens regularly:
J'ai français le jeudi. I have French on Thursdays.
Lucie joue au basket. Lucie is playing/plays basketball.

The present tense of regular -er verbs

Many French verbs end in *-er* in the infinitive. They take the same endings as *chanter* in the present tense:

(infinitive)	chanter	to sing
s (singular)	*je chante*	I sing/I am singing
	tu chantes	you sing/you are singing
	il chante	he sings/he is singing
	elle chante	she sings/she is singing
	on chante	we/they (people in general) sing/ we/they are singing
pl (plural)	*nous chantons*	we sing/we are singing
	vous chantez	you sing/you are singing
	ils chantent	they sing/they are singing
	elles chantent	they sing/they are singing

Other verbs in the present tense

Some of the most common (and useful!) verbs in French don't follow a pattern. Learn them by heart!

avoir	*être*	*faire*	*aller*
(to have)	(to be)	(to do; to make)	(to go)
j'ai	je suis	je fais	je vais
tu as	tu es	tu fais	tu vas
il a	il est	il fait	il va
elle a	elle est	elle fait	elle va
on a	on est	on fait	on va
nous avons	nous sommes	nous faisons	nous allons
vous avez	vous êtes	vous faites	vous allez
ils ont	ils sont	ils font	ils vont
elles ont	elles sont	elles font	elles vont

sortir	partir	pouvoir	vouloir
(to go out)	(to leave)	(can; to be able to)	(to want)
je sors	je pars	je peux	je veux
tu sors	tu pars	tu peux	tu veux
il sort	il part	il peut	il veut
elle sort	elle part	elle peut	elle veut
on sort	on part	on peut	on veut
nous sortons	nous partons	(For plural endings; see	
vous sortez	vous partez	*Formule X* Book 2)	
ils sortent	ils partent		
elles sortent	elles partent		

Notes

– Except for *avoir* and *être*, verbs which don't follow the same pattern as *chanter* have the same endings for *je* and for *tu*. For example:
je peux/tu peux; *je sors/tu sors*, etc.

– *Sortir* and *partir* are very similar to each other, as are *pouvoir* and *vouloir*. Learn them well!

Les phrases négatives – Negative sentences
◀◀ *to Formule X pp52, 63*

● To make an English sentence negative, you need to add in something either before <u>or</u> after the verb:
I am <u>not</u> patient   We <u>don't</u> like sciences

● In French, you need to put something before the verb (*ne* or *n'*) <u>and</u> something after it (*pas*):
Je ne *suis* pas *patient*
Nous n'*aimons* pas *les sciences*

● See *Les articles* p 53 about the use of *de* or *d'* for 'not any'.

Les questions – Questions
◀◀ *to Formule X p102*

Yes/no questions

To ask a question, you can use a question mark when you are writing something, or you can raise your intonation towards the end of a sentence when you are speaking:
Tu travailles? Are you working?

Useful question words

où where	*Tu habites où?*
qui who	*C'est qui?*
quand when	*C'est quand, ton anniversaire?*
pourquoi why	*Tu préfères le sport? Pourquoi?*
comment how	*Ça s'écrit comment?*
quel/quelle which	*C'est quelle page? Et quel exercice?*
qu'est-ce que what	*Qu'est-ce que c'est? Un cobaye?*
à quelle heure at what time	*Tu vas au cinéma à quelle heure?*

Other tips on questions

- You can use *AnneXe* to make a list of the useful questions you tend to forget.

- You will learn more ways of asking questions in *Formule X* Books 2 and 3.

Accents, cédilles, etc. – Accents, cedillas, etc.

Accents, cedillas, apostrophes and hyphens are important parts of learning to spell in French.

Accents

To be able to spell words when you are speaking (sometimes useful in lessons), learn what accents are called:

-é- = -e- accent aigü
-è- = -e- accent grave (-à- and -ù- also exist)
-ê- = -e- accent circomflexe (-â-, -î-, -ô- and -û- also exist)

Examples:
décembre - règle - à Leeds - où - bête - âge - s'il te plaît - drôle - août

Note the difference:

a/à	*Elle **a** une maison **à** Paris.*
	She has a house in Paris.

ou/où	*Tu habites **où**? A Toulouse **ou** à Nice?*
	Where do you live? In Toulouse or in Nice?

Cedillas

-ç- = -c- cédille

Cedillas can change the pronunciation of a word, and are sometimes used with words containing the letter *c*. See the difference a cedilla can make in the examples below:
– the sound *-ca-* in ca*ssette* is like the sound in 'camel'.
– the sound *-ça-* in *ça va* is like the sound in 'salmon'.

The letter *-œ-*

-œ- = -e- dans l'o

In a few French words, like *sœur* and *œuf*, these two vowels are joined to each other.

Apostrophes

- In French, apostrophes aren't used in the same way that we use them in English, so don't use them for the same purposes.

- Apostrophes with verbs:

In English, you can use…	…but in French, you don't have a choice!
I am quiet <u>or</u> I'm quiet	*Je suis calme*
I have a cat <u>or</u> I've a cat	*J'ai un chat* (*Je ai* doesn't exist)
He is small <u>or</u> He's small	*Il est petit*

- For other notes on apostrophes, see *La possession* (Using de/d') on p 54.

Hyphens

Hyphens are also important for spelling in French. Examples:
dix-sept seventeen
Rendez-vous à 2h00 Let's meet at 2.00
un demi-frère one step-brother
un milk-shake a milk shake
mes grands-parents my grandparents
cet après-midi this afternoon
qu'est-ce que c'est? what is it?
le centre-ville the town centre

à l'aide de	with the help of
Cache…	Hide…
Chante…	Sing…
Choisis…	Choose…
Classe…	Classify…/List…
Complète…	Complete…
correctement	correctly
Corrige…	Correct…
Décris…	Describe…
dessin	drawing
Devine…	Guess…
Dis…	Say…
Donne…	Give…
Écoute…	Listen to…
Écris…	Write…
Fais…	Do…
Fais correspondre…	Match up…
Imite…	Imitate…
Invente…	Make up…/Invent…
Joue…	Play…
Lis…/Lis à haute voix…	Read…/Read aloud…
de mémoire	from memory
Montre…	Point to…
mot	word
nom	name; noun
nombre	number
oralement	orally; in speaking
Pose des questions…	Ask questions…
Pratique…	Practise…
Prépare…	Prepare…
Qu'est-ce que…?	What…?
Recommence…	Start again…
Recopie…	Copy out…
Réécoute…	Listen again…
Regarde…	Look at…
Répète…	Repeat…
Réponds…	Answer…/Reply…
seul(e)	alone
Traduis…	Translate…
Travaille…	Work…
Trouve…	Find…
Vérifie…	Check…
vite (plus vite)	fast (faster)
vrai ou faux?	true or false?